CW00793725

THE BRIGHTON ROCK

PICTURE BOOK

THE MAKING OF THE
BOULTING BROTHERS FILM 1946-48

Màire McQueeney

MÀIRE MCQUEENEY

DINING TABLE PUBLICATIONS

For Patrick, my brother

(1943-1990)

First published in 1999 by
DINING TABLE PUBLICATIONS
22 Warleigh Road, Brighton BN1 4NT
Telephone 01273-607910
Email mcq20cwalk@mistral.co.uk.

Photo Credits:
Brighton Rock Stills © Canal+Image UK Limited,
Pinewood Studios, Iver, Bucks.

Picture Acknowledgements:
Canal + Image UK Ltd., British Film Institute Stills, Posters & Design,
National Film Television & Video Archive and Carol Marsh.

Text Acknowledgements:
Now My Heart Is Full
Words and Music By Steven Morrissey and Martin Boorer
© 1993 Bona Relations Ltd.
Warner/Chappell Music Ltd, London W6 8BS
Reproduced by IMP Ltd.

Front Cover Captions:
Filming on Palace Pier
1948 Cinema Poster

ISBN 0 9516085 4 1
Fonts Univers, Bembo and Gill Sans
Design by White Design
Scanning by Service 24
Printed by Redwood Books, Trowbridge.

CONTENTS

ACKNOWLEDGEMENTS

BEFORE I had lived in Brighton 3 years I knew that I would offer a seaside excursion exploring the imaginary geographic region created in Graham Greene's novel *Brighton Rock*. Taking a look at Greene and The Boulting Brothers' cinematic collaboration has taken considerably longer.

I am grateful to all of those named and unnamed who generously provided information, opinion, conversation, and practical support in assembling the materials used in *The Brighton Rock Picture Book*, especially:

Frank Gray of the Southeast Film and Video Archive, John Heron of Canal Plus Image UK Ltd. and Mandy of the British Film Institute Stills Library.

Roy Boulting, David Knowles, Carol Marsh, Jill Knowles Silverside, Peter Graham Scott, the late Jack Tinker, Percy Upton, Brenda Blaschke Weber, and the uncredited caption writer of the BFI Stills collection, for their memories of 1947.

Stephen Chibnall of the British Cinema and Television Research Group at De Montford University, Stephen Plaice writer in residence on the Hanover Herald Online Project, Roger Mead retired Assistant Chief Constable East Sussex Police Force, David J. Knowles and Patrick Morrisey for permission to quote from their published & unpublished work.

Professor Cedric Watts, Quentin Falk and Gene Phillips SJ and W.J. West for the guidance of their works on the cinema of Graham Greene.

Rob Fraser of Brighton & Hove Conservation Team, Albert Bullock historian of Palace Pier, film maker Jack Pizzey and Leanne Jarrett.

For their encouragement and brilliant detail: Adrian Slack of Brighton Festival, Fred Grey of the

LEFT HUNTED MAN FRED HALE ON EXTERIOR PUB SET IN WELWYN STUDIO. IN MARKET SQUARE. MEETING HOUSE LANE. NEAR UNION STREET. NORTH STREET.

University of Sussex CCE, Neil Sinyard of Hull University, Alan Burton of The British Cinema and Television Archive, John Roles & Rebecca Quinton of Brighton & Hove Museum, Roger Watkins of The Graham Greene Birthplace Trust, Anna Fudge, Sue Hadfield, Lars Hesse, Mr. Weller of Nelson Place, Jeannette Eddisford & Jeremy Kidd, Trevor Chepstow, Paul Welch, James Morrison and Cllr Joyce Edmond-Smith, Robin Morley, Jane Launchbury, Fr David Wostenholm who supported the Hanover Community Association Arts 4 Everyone Project which prompted the research for this book.

Ron Munro's tourism students at Brighton College of Technology, Jim Beavis (punter), the International Association of Teachers of English as a Foreign Language, The Crime Writers Association and the staff of HMV, Brighton who sourced the song Now My Heart is Full from the lyric Dallow, Spicer, Pinkie, Cubitt.

and lastly, Godfrey Smith of The Sunday Times who has encouraged my 20th Century Walks & my husband Mike Strong and the Strong family's long memories of Brighton.

ABOVE **WILLIAM 'BILLY' HARTNELL AND RICHARD ATTENBOROUGH WITH STAR CHAIRS AT WELWYN STUDIO. ATTENBOROUGH SHOWS OFF A COSMETICALLY 'LACED' CHEEK TO HIS FATHER, F. L. ATTENBOROUGH, PRINCIPAL OF LEICESTER UNIVERSITY COLLEGE. GREENE'S SCREENPLAY RECOMMENDS LEICESTER AS A PLACE TO SETTLE DOWN WITH THE £300 'APPEASEMENT' OFFERED BY COLLEONI.**

INTRODUCTION

"among the most truly cinematic British films of its time."

ALEXANDER WALKER, FILM CRITIC 1979.

BRIGHTON ROCK is the story of the last weeks in the life of Graham Greene's monstrous creation, seventeen year old Pinkie Brown. The illustrations in this book come from the film *Brighton Rock* produced by Roy Boulting, directed by the late John Boulting and photographed by the late Harry Waxman.

Imagine my surprise to discover Pinkie's face, in the image of the young Dickie Attenborough, looming large high over the concourse of Victoria Station in November 1997. According to Cam Winstanley of Total Film, it marked an unprecedented choice of a "Retro" British film to represent their international survey of the violent crime genre. Over the years *Brighton Rock*, a famous participant in the post-war 'spiv cycle', has been dubbed 'film noir' and acknowledged by Lord Attenborough as the beginning of his cinematic life of crime.

50th anniversary celebrations of the movie, which premiered locally in January 1948, increased my interest in examining the Brighton of the Boulting Brothers' film. Mythology holds that *Brighton Rock* was mostly filmed on location. This minor misconception is likely to persist along with the heresy that Brighton was a small fishing village when in 1783 the Prince of Wales first patronized horse racing on Whitehawk Down.

Publicity photos were plentiful in the studio archive but my search for the real Brighton of the film was frustrated until Frank Gray of the Southeast Film and Video Archive stepped in to help obtain frame stills. With the cooperation of John Heron of Canal Plus Image UK Ltd. and Anne Fleming of The British Film Institute Frank undertook to photograph the opening reel of the sole surviving safety print of *Brighton Rock*. Twenty images from the sequence which Phil Hardy dubs, "a stylistic tour de force" appear for the first time in this book.

Thirty years ago BBC Television's Omnibus series broadcast *The Hunted Man*, a three part programme celebrating the elusive man of letters Graham Greene. In the confines of an Orient Express carriage, Christopher Burstall interviewed the exiled writer. Greene's novel *Stamboul Train*, filmed by Twentieth Century Fox and released in 1934 under the title *Orient Express*, was the opening credit of his career as property provider to world cinema.

As they slowly rolled towards Istanbul Greene revealed that for him the Balkans had always been an area of infinite possibilities, but he thought Brighton had taken its place. *Brighton Rock* is a Byzantine mosaic of a story which wholly captures its time. Ante bellum Brighton revisited after the holocaust reveals the spirit of the first days when the word peace became a euphemism for Cold War. New modes of social, political and economic faith were claiming loyalty previously reserved for orthodox religion.

Where an age of prudence was needed to cope with the mass media's information overload, the divisive atomic age mushroomed instead. Even international cinema was temporarily stricken by the socialist versus capitalist Atlee-Truman showdown. Believing only the reality presented to them by the Daily Messenger, *Brighton Rock*'s unobservant Delia and Molly sat on Palace Pier waiting for Kolly Kibber.

66*Brighton Rock rocks*99

TOTAL FILM, MADFELLAS SUPPLEMENT NOVEMBER 1997.

RIGHT AT THE CLOCKTOWER. AT STATION BUS TERMINAL. MOBSTERS JOHNNIE AND CUBITT AT BRIGHTON STATION. FRED ON NO. 40 BUS ON QUEENS ROAD. FRED LOOKING OVER HIS SHOULDER FOR PURSUERS.

IN THE BEGINNING WAS THE WORD

"This were a fine reign:
To do ill and not to hear of it again."

THE WITCH OF EDMONTON

EPIGRAM TO THE NOVEL BRIGHTON ROCK

GREENE began a new thriller in the summer of 1936, soon after Paramount studios in Hollywood acquired the film rights to *A Gun for Sale*. This espionage story set in the Balkans, London and Nottwich (a fictional Nottingham) introduced the death of Battling Kite, a hoodlum, eliminated by James Raven and razor wielding confederates. The novelist chose a seaside setting for his follow up and felt he had an excellent title in *Brighton Rock*.

Graham Greene attended Brighton races on Tuesday August 4th 1936 the day after the News Chronicle's circulation publicist 'Lobby Lud' visited the town distributing his valuable cards. He dared newspaper readers to see what was in front of their eyes by dining at Forte's. Greene's research produced a violent parable of the detection of crime and the forgiveness of sin set against a background of racecourse gang warfare. The conviction of the "Hoxton Mob" at Lewes Assises court had made headlines in July 1936.

Although not an immediate hit in the summer of 1938 London's Evening Standard serialized *Brighton Rock* in September as Britain faced the Munich Crisis. A Penguin paperback edition followed in 1939. 80,000 copies were sold, to the chagrin of Brighton Borough Council. During the war Frank Harvey wrote a stage play with Greene communicating his misgivings from Freetown, Sierra Leone. The play starred nineteen year old Richard Attenborough as Sussex teenager Pinkie Brown and Hermoine Baddeley as Ida Arnold.

After the war the novel's film rights were acquired by partners Bill Linnit, Anatole de Grunwald and playwright Terence Rattigan. The story had a central concern that 'Right be done' which connected with Rattigan's latest stage play *The Winslow Boy*. His screenplay for *Brighton Rock* was intended to be a Screen International production directed by Anthony Asquith. However, by high summer of 1946 the rights had been sold to Charter Film Productions for £12,000. John Boulting took over the direction of the film which would be financed by the Associated British Picture Corporation, partly owned by the American studio Warner Brothers.

The Rattigan version focused on the devil and offset Ida's easy heterosexual virtue against Pinkie's perceived carnal solitude. Graham Greene had been consulting with his adapter Rattigan and neither of them found the script wholly to their liking. Greene wrote an independent film play to explore his vision of a poetic cinema with deep truths underlying the moving images. It contracted the geography of the book and kept the suggestion that Pinkie's marriage was consummated. The writers shared a £6,000 fee and Greene received the leading credit on the film. It is tantalizing to wonder how many subtle changes to the texture of the story were contributed by Rattigan who in later years made his home on Marine Parade in Kemptown.

Highlights of Greene's long association with the town included 'goat carting' and discovering the beguiling magic of moving pictures. He never forgot the excitement of encountering Anthony Hope's heroine *Sophy of Kravonia* on the silver screen in Brighton in 1911.

By curious co-incidence ten years later identical twin brothers John and Roy Boulting also watched their first movie in Brighton. They visited The Regent on North Street a splendid new picture palace showing Rex Ingram's silent classic *The Four Horseman of the Apocalypse*. Heady stuff for 8 year olds but Nanny loved Valentino! The theatre, which seated 1,700, was locally held to be "the largest, finest, most artistic kinematograph establishment in the country, if not in the world." Roy Boulting remembers that day as a transformation, a road to Damascus experience, perhaps the moment that he and John became film makers.

In 1946 the invitation from the Boulting Brothers resulted in the finest adaptation of Greene's serious fiction and was, for him, the first of three cinematic steps leading to the Grand Prix at Cannes in 1950.

> "Brighton Rock *is an utterly distinctive minor masterpiece, part thriller, part detective story, part satiric fantasy and part theological riddle.*"
>
> CEDRIC WATTS,
> A PREFACE TO GREENE

LEFT DIRECTOR JOHN BOULTING AT WELWYN STUDIO WITH WRITER GRAHAM GREENE AND ACTOR NIGEL STOCK IN SPIV COSTUME AS THE GANGSTER CUBITT FOR HIS FILM DEBUT.

CINEMA JUBILEE 1946

We have managed to produce a score of worthwhile films this year. Indeed some of these are among the best motion pictures ever made anywhere.

PETER NOBLE, INTRODUCTION BRITISH FILM YEAR BOOK 1947-48

PEACE came to England in 1945 with great promise of change. The Labour landslide in the General Election lead to the establishment in April 1948 of a National Health Service in time to welcome much of the increased postwar birthrate remembered as "the baby boom". A little earlier wartime cinema attendances had also boomed.

Although studio facilities, film stock and the tools of the trade were in short supply the British film industry produced 'home product' of increasing technical skill, prestige and box office appeal.

1946, the jubilee year, acknowledged the pioneering days of 1896 when film makers successfully exhibited moving images to an appreciative public in Paris, London, New York, Brighton and Hove. Exhibitors saw the highest cinema attendance figures ever recorded in England.

London's Daily Mail celebrated the co-incidence of its own jubilee by introducing the National Film Award Ballot. To bridge the gap between war and peace films released between September 3rd 1939 and September 3rd 1945 were included in the newspaper's film poll. On March 3rd the first British Film Festival opened at London's Leicester Square Theatre, with an audience of 2,000 for the presentation of the Daily Mail's National Film Awards. Despite the popularity and dominance of American films in UK cinemas, over 500,000 readers voted James Mason and Margaret Lockwood, the stars of Leslie Arliss' *The Wicked Lady*,

LEFT FRED HALE ON FOOT AGAIN IN NORTH ROAD. CHURCH STREET. MARLBOROUGH PLACE. crossing towards ROYAL PAVILION NORTH GATE. passing POLICE OFFICER, RUNNING TOWARDS SEAFRONT.

as best actor and actress. Curiously, the nominations were illustrated by theatrical tableau on the stage instead of today's ubiquitous film clips.

They awarded best film to director Anthony Asquith's *The Way to the Stars* with a screenplay by Terence Rattigan. That same team headed by producer Anatole De Grunwald was busy planning their next major motion picture, the adaptation of Graham Greene's novel *Brighton Rock*.

Accolades for British cinema arrived from several continents. The new International Film Festival at Cannes judged David Lean's *Brief Encounter* the outstanding film from any country in 1946. The New York Film Critics selected *Brief Encounter*'s star Celia Johnson as best actress awarding best actor to Laurence Olivier for his performance as *Henry V*. In October the Festival of British Film in Prague was promoted in the spirit of normalizing international trade.

Meanwhile, back at Buckingham Palace, King George VI and Queen Elizabeth had commanded that a performance of Michael Powell & Emeric Pressburger's *A Matter of Life and Death* (USA *Stairway to*

ABOVE **FORMER EVENING ARGUS CRIME REPORTER FRED HALE (ALAN WHEATLY) SHARES A TENSE MOMENT WITH SEASIDE ENTERTAINER IDA ARNOLD (HERMIONE BADDELEY) JUST A FEW MINUTES BEFORE HIS FATAL FALL FROM DANTE'S INFERNO. INTENSE ARTIFICIAL LIGHT WAS USED TO CREATE SUMMER ON THE PALACE PIER SET AT WELWYN STUDIO.**

Heaven) be shown at the Empire Theatre, Leicester Square. Three days later on the 4th of November a constitutional committee for the British Film Academy met to plan for the future in the face of the widely held belief that British and American cinema were divided by a common language.

BELOW JOHN BOULTING DIRECTS NEWLY-WEDS PINKIE BROWN (RICHARD ATTENBOROUGH) AND ROSE BROWN (CAROL MARSH) ARRIVING AT THE COSMOPOLITAN HOTEL FOR THEIR HONEYMOON. THIS LAVISH SET WAS THE FIRST EVER BUILT AT THE MGM BRITISH STUDIO IN BOREHAMWOOD.

Since late 1942 J. Arthur Rank, king of British cinema, was the acknowledged English ambassador to Hollywood with a mission to promote British film throughout the world. Rank was motivated both by the industry's economic necessity and his own evangelical zeal. A glowing memory of the success enjoyed in America by Alexander Korda's *The Private Life of Henry VIII* remained. That production starring Charles Laughton had cost well under £100,000. It opened at Radio City Music Hall, New York in October 1933 and grossed over half a million pounds during its first world run.

Rank had negotiated a Lend Lease plan under which British actors would occasionally make films for Universal International in Hollywood. America's box office generated 10 times the revenue

of Britain's domestic market and provided powerful cash incentives to European actors, directors and technicians as soon as post war travel restrictions were lifted. American distributors enjoyed free access to British cinema audiences. £18,000,000 of box office receipts were exported to America during 1946 and UK box office was considered essential to support the profitability of Hollywood studios.

The post war privation of domestic and industrial rationing was deepened when the winter of 1946-7 turned out to be the worst in living memory. Fuel shortages lead to domestic power being banned 5 hours a day. Bread rationing and the untypical winter freeze increased demand for black market goods. The heyday of the wideboy and spiv racketeer had arrived. Audiences continued to flock to the flicks but slowly numbers fell as many sporting fixtures returned to the social calendar and baby sitting became a national preoccupation.

Powell & Pressburger's *A Matter of Life and Death* (USA *Stairway to Heaven*) which had the honour of being shown before their Majesties The King and Queen as the first Royal Command performance, was

ABOVE THE MOBILE FILM UNIT PREPARES WITH ACTOR ALAN WHEATLEY, IN COSTUME AS FRED HALE, FOR HIS RUN THROUGH THE LANES AND NORTH LAINE.

both surreal and supernatural (Richard Attenborough, recently demobbed from the RAF Film Unit, played a British airman). Box office successes on both sides of the Atlantic featured comforting messages of survival in paradise.

Cinema jubilee year ended with exceptional premiers including Peter Ustinov's radar boffin movie *School for Secrets* featuring, among its distinguished cast, Richard Attenborough as a young pilot. He had also been cast as Andrews for Sydney & Muriel Box's adaptation of Graham Greene's 19th century Sussex adventure *The Man Within*, a Gainsborough Picture retitled *The Smugglers* for US release.

BELOW LOCATION FILMING ON BRIGHTON SEAFRONT EAST OF THE GRAND HOTEL WHERE THE BRIGHTON CENTRE STANDS TODAY. THE CAMERA RECORDS A BRIEF SCENE OF TENACIOUS AMATEUR GUMSHOE IDA TRACKING DOWN WITNESSES MOLLY & DELIA.

Richard Attenborough and his wife Sheila Sim were under contract to Charter Films, the independent production company which formalized the Boulting brothers working partnership. John Boulting, while an officer in the RAF Film Unit had directed *Journey Together* a 1945 documentary-feature written by Terence Rattigan showing how the RAF trained aircrews. It starred Hollywood actor Edward G. Robinson (see?) and featured A.C.1, R. Attenborough. The cameraman Harry Waxman and production designer John Howell would also be hired for the Boulting's production of *Brighton Rock*.

ABOVE **THE DIRECTOR IS BARE CHESTED WHILE ACTORS AND EXTRAS SWELTERED IN COSTUME DURING THE EXTRA- ORDINARY SUMMER OF 1947. NO LOCATION FILMING DAYS WERE LOST TO RAIN.**

RIGHT **PETER GRAHAM SCOTT'S ATMOSPHERIC USE OF DISSOLVES IS CAPTURED IN THIS FRAME STILL. PLEASURE BOAT SM 492 IS SURROUNDED BY THE SEA EVEN WHERE THE SKY OUGHT TO BE.**

ON THE TOWN 1947

"*Sussex's premier resort may be popularly known as 'London-by-the-sea' but in the imagination of film-makers it is more specifically 'Soho-on-sea'*".

STEVE CHIBNALL, 'PURGATORY AT THE END OF THE PIER: IMPRINTING A SENSE OF PLACE THROUGH *BRIGHTON ROCK*' IN THE FAMILY WAY: THE BOULTING BROTHERS AND BRITISH FILM CULTURE.

ROY Boulting, having directed *Fame is the Spur* for Fillipo Del Giudici's Two Cities Films, took the role of producer for *Brighton Rock* and with it the unusual step of revisiting the Sussex Coast to scout for film locations. The 'talkies' introduced a need for sound stages and all but killed location filming. But, documentary making in emergency war conditions had taught some techniques for straightforward dealing with the natural world to record life as it happens. The Boultings were anticipating a trend.

Although born in Bray, Berkshire John and Roy Boulting lived on Hove's New Church Road where, as youngsters, they were propagandized to believe neighbouring Brighton was 'Sin City' fit only to pass through quickly in transit. Combining the Boultings' resident appreciation of the odd fraternal twin towns, sinful Brighton and hallowed Hove with Greene's acute perceptions was a master stroke which resulted in the most influential vision of an English town ever captured on celluloid.

The brothers' professional partnership began late in 1937 when John returned from his service as a front line ambulance driver with the International Brigade in Spain. Hitler's war interrupted commercial film

LEFT THE CAMERA ABANDONED FRED FOR A DRAMATIC VIEW TOWARDS THE SHORE. FRED OUTSIDE THE PALACE OF FUN. IN DANTE'S INFERNO A BLIND MAN AND HIS GRANDDAUGHTER WITNESS MURDER, BUT CAN'T SEE PINKIE'S SELF SATISFIED SMIRK. A GHOUL HEIGHTENS THE EXPRESSIONISM OF THE SEQUENCE. PINKIE BROWN IS THE CALM FACE OF EVIL.

making, but by 1946 they were back in harness alternating the roles of producer/director, establishing their reputation as key British film makers.

Early in 1947, while throughout the country film studios were taken out of mothballs and stages re-equipped, Roy Boulting was collecting local Brighton characters and testing the prevailing temperament of a borough council not best pleased by the image of the town presented in Greene's very successful pre-war novel. His talent spotting discovered Carl Ramon, former razor man with the London based Sabini gang, who was hired as both 'technical advisor' and actor.

John Boulting worked with Associated British Picture Corporation's executive producer Warwick Ward to recreate Brighton in Welwyn Garden City. Art director John Howell designed sets including The Four Feathers Public House, Brighton Police Station, Palace Pier, Snow's Cafe and Princes Dance Hall, which is never named in the film. Costume designer Honoria Plesch, who had worked with Oliver Messell on *The Thief of Bagdad*, had the unenviable job of finding

ABOVE JIM (UNKNOWN) LANDLORD OF THE FOUR FEATHERS, CHALKS UP LETTERS ON THE BAR WHILE TURF ACCOUNTANT PHIL CORKERY (GEORGE CARNEY) CALLS TIME WHEN IDA REACHES AN X. BETWEEN SHOWS WITH A COSTUMED PIERROT TROUPE, IDA ARNOLD EXERCISES HER PSYCHIC SKILLS ON THE EVENING GAZETTE.

ABOVE **MUSIC OF THE BIG BAND STIRS THE AIR AND THE SOULS OF THE DANCERS WHILE A WAITRESS SLUMPS WEARILY AGAINST THE WALL. PINKIE AND ROSE SIT AND SPEAK OF HEAVEN, HELL, ATHEISTS AND ROSARY BEADS AS ROSE EATS ICE CREAM FROM A SUNDAE DISH CHALICE. A WOMAN DANCING ON THE RIGHT IS WEARING TROUSERS, QUITE 'FAST' FOR 1937. THE ORCHESTRAL ARRANGEMENT IN THIS SCENE MARKED JOHN ADDISON'S FILM DEBUT.**

materials to recreate 1930s fashion when the originals had been worn to rags during years of "utility fashion". The £178,000 budget was also applied to casting with the major roles going to the actors who created the main characters Pinkie, Dallow, Spicer, Ida and Prewitt, on stage in 1943. The exception was Rose, the girl from Nelson Place, originally played by Dulcie Gray.

Jack Worrow, the film's publicist had the job of grabbing newspaper headlines for the production and succeeded by instituting a national talent search for a teenaged actress to play Rose. Over 3,000 applications were received but the role went to newcomer Carol Marsh strongly recommended by Olive Dodds of the J. Arthur Rank Organization's Charm School in Highbury.

Actress Carol Marsh's film career began in bed alone on the set of Pinkie's room at Frank's Place. The production was already underway when she joined the cast in Welwyn Studio in April 1947 shortly before her 19th birthday. Her Roman Catholic convent school education had been expanded as a drama scholar at The Royal Academy of Music and followed by a brief six weeks at Rank's famous charm school. Brenda Blaschke Weber who now makes her home in Brighton fondly remembers Carol as, "sweet, natural and a hard worker completely lacking in star pretensions" despite the daunting publicity which surrounded her film debut.

Brenda Blaschke aged 15 travelled from London to Welwyn Studio for open auditions on the "ifit", theatrical jargon for "che sera, sera". She and her friend Gloria Jordan were hired as extras and paid a premium wage for wearing their own clothes. Brenda's enduring contribution to the film's atmosphere was as the 'screamer' in the sound track for the ghost train, a scene filmed in a shed in Southend by young film editor Peter Graham Scott.

Dante's Inferno was pure expressionist invention. Palace Pier never hosted such a poetically named ride. Scott gratefully remembers the Boultings' "Quixotic nature" which approved such independence and technical experimentation for the suspenseful murder scene. On location, Scott launched a camera off Palace Pier to achieve the dizzying victim's eye view of death between the devil and the deep blue sea.

Fred Hale's terrified run through Brighton was added to the story for the film cameras. Harry Waxman recorded The Lanes and North Laine with a punchiness that keeps the audience struggling with Fred every step of the way. In places 'stolen' filming from a hidden camera replaced

BELOW **BETRAYAL BY PINKIE TRIGGERED A RAZOR ATTACK ON SPICER. RACECOURSE EVANGELIST (NORMAN WATSON) IS LOST IN THE CROWD BUT HIS PLACARD WARNING, "THE WAGES OF SIN IS DEATH", CAN BE SEEN ON THE TURF IN THE CENTRE OF THE PICTURE. BRIGHTON'S GUNN FAMILY ARE REPRESENTED AS BOOKMAKERS.**

ABOVE PINKIE INCESSANTLY CONTORTS THE CAT'S CRADLE STRING DESPITE HIS SLASHED AND BANDAGED HAND. RICHARD ATTENBOROUGH INTRODUCED THIS NERVOUS PRAYERFUL GESTURE INTO HIS STAGE CREATION OF PINKIE BROWN IN 1943. CROOKED LAWYER PREWITT (HARCOURT WILLIAMS) OFFERS PINKIE EXPENSIVE COUNSEL ON MARRIAGE LAWS AND CUSTOMS. WILLIAMS TAUGHT BOTH ATTENBOROUGH AND NIGEL STOCK DURING THEIR STUDENT DAYS AT THE ROYAL ACADEMY OF DRAMATIC ARTS.

the mobile film unit but Peter Self of Peacehaven remembers innocently strolling through a scene conspicuously lit with floodlights. Unselfconcious boys running on Church Street and women with coach built prams obligingly provided glimpses of every day life totally indifferent to Fred's nightmare of pursuit.

In the second of the Evening Argus supplements to mark the 50th anniversary of the film, distinguished film maker Lord Attenborough, recently created Chancellor of the University of Sussex, offered a few historic technical insights: "in those days films were in black and white, and the 'size' the cinema picture was in was what used to be called an academic ratio, which was a lot more narrow than today. The whole dimensions of the screen have totally changed over the years, so that now, when you want to show vast areas you can use a wide screen to film huge plains, but back then even an ordinary broad road was hard to fit in the picture. Given that problem the narrow Lanes were a dream." Carol Marsh remembers young Attenborough as a crysallis film maker who encouraged her to look through the camera lens and see acting from the audience's point of view.

BELOW **At Frank's Place the remains of Kite's Mob celebrate Pinkie's marriage to Rose. Cubitt sits cross-legged playing with one doll while Dallow (William Hartnell) snogs another. Judy (Victoria Winter) holds the hand of her blind husband Frank (Reginald Purdell). The kiss is fleeting on the screen.**

RIGHT "BOGIES" ON THE LOWER JETTY OF PALACE PIER WITH IDA AND DALLOW AT THE HOUR OF PINKIE'S DEATH. 1930S BRIGHTON POLICE OFFICERS ACTUALLY WORE WHITE HELMETS DURING THE SUMMER MONTHS. IN THE CHIARASCURO LIGHTING IDA'S COSTUME OF FUR JACKET, SUEDE GLOVES AND HAT SUGGESTS EITHER A FASHION CONSCIOUS PERFORMER OR AN EVIL "GOAT OF MENDES" WITH THE HORNS OF THE DEVIL.

The use of 'overflow' studio space at MGM (British) Studios Ltd. (formerly Amalgamated Studios) was unexceptional but notable as the Cosmo sets were the first ever built there. Soon actor Ronald Reagan would visit "Elstree, the British Hollywood" as co-star of *The Hasty Heart*. But not before the Atlee government imposed a drastic 75% Ad Valorem Tax on film imports. America responded in August 1947 with an embargo on British films which lasted seven months. A.P.B.C., eager to exhibit in Warner Brothers' 3,000 US cinemas, had not required actors to produce an authentic Brighton accent.

Roy Boulting made a friend's home in Ovingdean his headquarters for producing a shooting script in close association with Graham Greene. Essential cast and crew arrived in Brighton late in June to begin their 8 week shoot during the hottest summer on record. The Grand Hotel was production headquarters and home to the major stars. Carol Marsh, twelfth in the films credit's, stayed at The Metropole and being under contract to Rank was responsible for her own expenses. Christopher Law, Richard Attenborough's stunt double, and other crew billeted in Sillwood Lodge in Hove.

Earlier that month, 18 year old blonde beauty queen Jill Knowles won the title Miss Brighton plus a bit part in the film – another very successful publicity stunt anticipating the crews arrival in town. Jill's fondest memories are reserved for Hermione Baddeley. Universally called "Totie", she mothered the 'special' film extras in her luxurious suite in the Grand. Jill recalls the excitment of the crowds needed for race scenes and the drama when Alderman S. C. Thompson ordered the film unit off Brighton racecourse. They had overstayed their three day licence. An appeal to Brighton Council ensured that filming continued.

Personal appearances were in demand all over town both night and day. Jill Knowles Silverside, as she is now known, remembers the glamour of the *Brighton Rock* dance competition at Sherry's Dance Hall on West Street attended by Brighton's mayor Percy Friend-James and the lady mayoress. Starlet Carol Marsh, in evening dress, announced the winners and star "Dickie" Attenborough presented the awards. The cast had managed a special visit to Sussex County Hospital to sign autographs for the nurses as well.

LEFT TEENAGED WIDOW ROSE BROWN OFFERS EVIDENCE OF PINKIE'S LOVE IN THE REVISED SECOND ENDING FILMED FOR *BRIGHTON ROCK*. THE (UNKNOWN) NUN IS ADDRESSED AS MOTHER.

Graham Greene's intense life was at a pitch of complexity in the summer of 1947. His past included a brief membership of the Communist Party and a longer relationship with MI6. Bill West's complex study *The Quest for Graham Greene* describes how potential scandal shadowed his life and work. Fatefully, he visited *Brighton Rock* on location with his lover Dorothy Glover whom he introduced, by her pen name, as illustrator Dorothy Craigie. Few people knew of their very private long standing affair but one of the crew recognised the lovers. The gossip reached Catherine Walston, a wealthy married American who had asked the famous writer to be her sponsor when she joined the Church of Rome the year before. They had been intimate friends ever since. The scandal of the married Roman Catholic writer with a live-in lover plus a mistress, who was his god daughter, cast the sundry shenanigans of actors and film makers on the town in "sin city" into a deep shade.

IN THE CAN 1948

"Brighton is now a film star."

EVENING NEWS JANUARY 1948

BELOW **ATTENBOROUGH AT WELWYN STUDIO WITH TECHNICAL ADVISOR CARL RAMON WHO CARRIED A RAZOR FOR THE LONDON BASED SABINI GANG. RAMON'S ASSOCIATION WITH THE FILM IS UNCREDITED DESPITE HIS BRIEF BUT EFFECTIVE APPEARANCE AS CHARLIE THE BARMAN.**

B*RIGHTON ROCK* premiered at The Savoy Cinema on East Street at Midnight January 8th 1948 with an invited celebrity audience in the stalls and ticket holding star-struck Brightonians in the packed gallery. The stars came on stage to wild applause with the exception of Carol Marsh who was in Paris filming *Alice in Wonderland*, directed by Lou Bunin.

One of the John Boulting's young crew had fancied himself the Orson Welles of England. Shots of Fred Hale's running feet suggest Welles' tour de force *Citizen Kane* and anticipate famous scenes of Harry Lime's shoe leather in Carol Reed's *The Third Man*.

Post censorship, the film which debuted that midnight was still the story of Brighton's Pinkie Brown, a sadistic Boy befriended by William

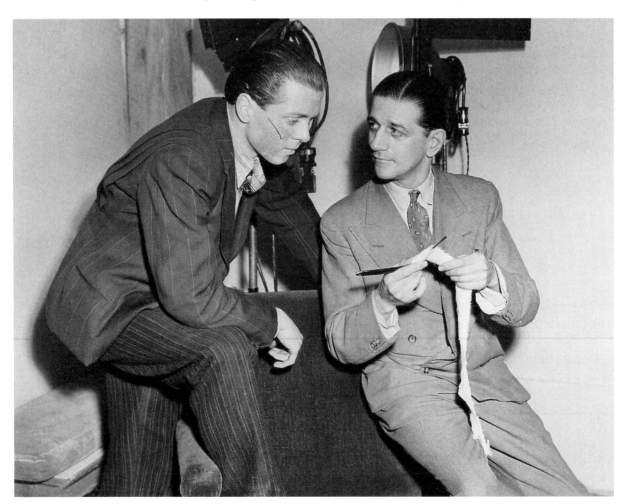

Kite's mob, who unhesitatingly revenges his mentor's betrayal and callous mutilation despite the threat of capital punishment. Scapegoat journalist Fred Hale, in sunny Brighton as the Daily Messenger's publicist 'Kolly Kibber', is pursued through The Lanes and North Laine by Johnnie, Cubitt and Dallow. With a sweet spin on gangster argot Fred gets "taken for a ride" by Pinkie on Palace Pier crowded with thousands of day trippers. The police report on Fred's corpse obligingly shows that he died of a coronary. Far from being a hunted man on the run, 17 year old Pinkie openly conducts a whirlwind courtship of potential witness for the prosecution Rose, negotiates intermittently with crime godfather Colleoni, and cold bloodedly kills his pal Spicer in the space of two short weeks.

A recognizable Brighton of touring Pierrot parties, pleasure boats, seaside photographers and summer race meetings is the battlefield for a confrontation between information and understanding. Pinkie manipulatively plots a cynical double suicide with his loving new bride Rose Brown. Pursued by amateur detective Ida Arnold, his brief life of crime and his search for glory end with a plunge into stygian darkness

ABOVE **PINKIE AND DALLOW ARE MOTORISED GANGSTERS PAYING A MIDNIGHT COLLECTION VISIT TO BOOKMAKER BILL BREWER. THE BACKDROP IS PAINTED BUT THE FOREGROUND STRONGLY RESEMBLES HOUSING ON LEWES ROAD DEMOLISHED IN 1976.**

ABOVE **BREWER (HARRY ROSS) IS CARVED BY PINKIE FOR TRANSFERRING HIS "PROTECTION" PAYMENTS TO COLLEONI. GREENE LOCATES THIS VIOLENCE AT THE SITE OF THE 1926 'BATTLE OF LEWES ROAD', A CONFRONTATION DURING THE GENERAL STRIKE.**

from the lower landing stage of Palace Pier. Pinkie Brown's final question to Dallow is, "Why?"

All that remains of the Boy is his voice on his widow's sabotaged vulcanite disc and, just possibly, his immortal soul.

Newspaper reviews were mixed but mostly favourable with strong accolades for all the cast and the Boulting sincerity of direction and production. Reg Whitely film critic of the Daily Mirror famously issued an unprecedented two page condemnation of the film headlined: False, Nasty: Is This What You Want to See? He singled out the film's failure to put over the subtle religious theme of the novel. Graham Greene replied immediately lambasting the British Board of Film Censors for their part in refusing to permit Pinkie to speak words from the Roman Catholic Mass.

Privately Graham Greene was moved to agree with the critics that Attenborough was a 'perfect Pinkie' despite his initial misgivings. Greene's interest lay in what he called a poetic cinema in which not only the dialogue and camera angles but also the silences and postures deepened the sense of the film play. The urban space of real Brighton was the film's other star. Despite its reliance on film sets *Brighton Rock* achieved a rare vivacity.

Compare it, for instance, to Ealing's *Pink String and Sealing Wax*, a stiff 1945 rendition of Rowland Pertwee's stage play possibly inspired by Brighton's notorious 'Chocolate Box Murderess'.

The ante bellum Brighton invented by Greene and the Boultings is like a house of mirrors in the palace of fun where reality is distorted to both frighten and entertain. The only observers will be willing accomplices visiting the funfair, reading the entertainment, or sitting in the darkened cinema.

"The feelings of the town being represented" were paramount to the British Board of Film Censors. Roy Boulting feels the disclaimer which opens the film was justified to secure the cooperation he needed from town officials. The censor, Brooke Wilkinson, had required deletions of dialogue and a new ending to pass *Brighton Rock* with an Adult A certificate allowing children under 16 to attend with their parents. It still caused significant outrage for its image of Brighton and life in Britain when it opened at the Warner cinema in Leicester Square.

BELOW SUAVE GANGSTER COLLEONI (CHARLES GOLDNER) ADMIRES MR. P BROWN'S PUSHINESS. AN ENIGMATIC GOLDEN SPHINX DECORATES PINKIE'S STRIPPED REGENCY CHAIR. THE FICTIOUS COSMOPOLITAN HOTEL WAS MODELLED ON BRIGHTON'S BEDFORD WHICH BURNT DOWN IN 1964.

FILM REVIEWS 1948

◆ "*Brighton Rock* at the Warner Theatre, has been described as "false" and "nasty" I say it is a masterly production of an exciting story." W. A. WILCOX SUNDAY DISPATCH JANUARY 11TH.

◆ "the film is notable for the performances of Hermione Baddeley , who is downright magnificent as the "suicide blonde" (ie dyed by her own hand) and William Hartnell, surely one of the best actors on the screen as a gangster" JACK DAVIES SUNDAY EXPRESS JANUARY 11TH.

◆ "The film is splendidly directed for maximum thrills and character drawing and ideally cast with Richard Attenborough as the gangster, Hermione Baddeley as the soubrette, William Hartnell, Harcourt Williams, Wylie Watson and everyone else giving magnificent performances, to say nothing of a sensitive newcomer Carol Marsh as the unhappy heroine." EVENING NEWS JANUARY 8TH.

◆ "this well made, excellently acted film, with the imprint of Boulting sincerity, is not just one more story of the underworld. It is a serious analysis of spivery." JOAN LESTER REYNOLDS NEWS JANUARY 11TH.

BELOW THE POLICE INSPECTOR(CAMPBELL COPELIN) GIVES BROWN A FRIENDLY WARNING TO CLEAR OUT OF BRIGHTON, CONFIRMING THAT PINKIE HAS LITERALLY "GOT AWAY WITH MURDER". THE SET, MODELLED ON THE OLD BRIGHTON CENTRAL POLICE STATION IN THE BASEMENT OF TOWN HALL, INCLUDES A LARGE CLOCK TO UNDERSCORE THE FILM'S OBSESSION WITH TIME.

NODS AND WINKS

Here are a few nods and winks to look out for the next time you rent the video or see *Brighton Rock* on late night television.

◆ The film's ficticious Evening Argus headline 'Brighton Gangsters Body Found in Gravel Pit' carries the byline Peter Black, a real post war reporter for the Sussex newspaper based in Brighton.

◆ Peter Black's article about the discovery of the mutilated corpse of William Kite, 45, reveals that journalist Fred Hale was a former Argus crime reporter. So why did they shop him on the front page?

◆ Fred Hale's run up Queen's Road to Brighton Station took him past the Moon Unit of the RNIB, a publishing works specializing in embossed literature for the blind. The only other Moon Unit was in Los Angeles, California not far from Hollywood.

◆ Charlie the barman at the Four Feathers is played by Carl Ramon, former razor man with the London based Sabini gang.

◆ Ida Arnold's psychic conversation with the departed ends when her message reaches an X or a Z. Catholic convert Cardinal John Henry Newman used these symbols to allude to theological factions within the Church of England during the 1830s. They draw attention to Brighton's close association with the Oxford Movement for those who share Greene's keen interest in church history.

◆ Colleoni's employee benefits package included hospitalization, with grapes, very much in the style of Chicago gangster Al Capone.

◆ The police report on Fred Hale's death is dated Saturday June 9th, a date which occured in 1934, the year of the mysterious Brighton Trunk Murder.

◆ Mr. Al Parker, paged in the lobby of the Cosmoplitan Hotel, shared his name with a prominent theatrical agent who represented Attenborough, Hartnell and Copelin in the cast of *Brighton Rock*.

◆ Pinkie's muddle of a suicide pact, with pax, the Latin word meaning peace, was new dialogue for the film. The Boy's weak vocabulary draws attention to another of Graham Greene's interests, PAX, a political Roman Catholic peacetime development in Eastern Europe.

◆ Leicester, suggested as a fine place for the gang to relocate was the boyhood home of Richard Attenborough whose parents and brother David visited him at work on the *Brighton Rock* set.

◆ The camera lingers on 'Miss Brighton' and a brunette inspecting 'Todays Snaps' near Palace Pier just before Rose spots Spicer's photo.

"The day after the premier, with 7/6 burning a hole in my pocket, I went in search of a tartan tie- similar to the one worn by Pinkie in the film, and found one for just that price in a shop in St. James Street."

DAVID J. KNOWLES,
BITTERSWEET DAYS
1947.

CRIME & PUNISHMENT

"Crime in Brighton, with the exception of the notorious trunk murders and the agonizing suspense of the last minute reprieve of those who kidnapped and murdered the elderly Mr. Friend-Smith, was not in any way excessive. Every town has a criminal element and Brighton of the thirties was no exception. There is no evidence of any organised criminality in the town of any kind. The only organised crime element at the race course was without exception made up of visitors to the town."

ROGER MEAD, MA THESIS

BELOW DALLOW WITNESSES PINKIE PUSH SPICER(WYLIE WATSON) TO HIS DEATH THROUGH THE WEAK BANNISTER AT FRANK'S PLACE. HE REMAINS TRUE TO HIS YOUNG FRIEND EVEN OFFERING EYE-WITNESS EVIDENCE TO CUBITT THAT IT WAS DEFINITELY AN ACCIDENTAL DEATH.

From *The Waste Land*'s demotic invitation to a single sex weekend at the Metropole to *A Handful of Dust*'s unloving weekend for fake divorce evidence, the tourist attractions of pre war Brighton, captured in literature, highlighted the 'not strictly legal' for visitors with special

interests. The national press in 1928 headlined the commuted death sentence for Brightonians convicted of Mr. Friend-Smith's murder. With the two notorious Trunk Murders following in 1934, Brighton meant crime in the popular imagination.

Influential poet T.S. Eliot's religious verse pagent *The Rock* edified Londoners at Sadler's Wells Theatre in June 1934. Derby Day that year co-incided with an anonymous plywood trunk being deposited at Brighton Station left luggage. So in a week ending Saturday June 9th religion, racing and undetected cold blooded murder converged. The first trunk murder was finally discovered on June 17th when the headless torso was examined at Brighton Police Station.

Brighton Rock is obsessed with our reliance on proof and evidence to establish Truth. The theologian St. Thomas Aquinas taught that faith was given to us because our frail human senses could never lead us to perfect understanding without the grace of God. *Brighton Rock* is truly concerned with all things both visible and invisible with blindness a recurring motif in both the novel and film.

ABOVE **RICHARD ATTENBOROUGH ENJOYS ICE CREAM WITH YOUNG ADMIRERS ON THE LAWN OF BRIGHTON'S ROYAL PAVILION AT ONE OF MANY PERSONAL APPEARANCES REQUESTED OF THE VISITING FILM STARS. THE DISTINCTIVE HOUSES IN THE BACKGROUND ARE NUMBERS 3 & 4 OLD STEINE.**

Brighton Rock is a technology showcase with its photography, sound recordings, cars, telephones, mass circulation newspapers, fairground rides imported from Coney Island, and the one false note of Pinkie's hand gun. Brighton had proudly made police history in 1933 when officers were issued with wireless radios operated from a transmitter on the Town Hall roof. This rapid police communication is hinted at in the film. A detective waits like a doorman for Brown to exit from his meeting in the Cosmopolitan. The police car sweeps into the frame to drive Pinkie to help with enquiries, suggesting a taxi service requested by Mr. Colleoni and facilitated by the prototype 'mobile phone'.

BELOW BOOKMAKER PHIL CORKERY REWARDS THE FAITH OF PUNTERS WHO BACKED BLACK BOY IN THE FICTIOUS SATURDAY 4:00 RACE AT BRIGHTON. THE TIC TAC MEN MAKE SECRET SIGNALS.

Never the scene of serious gang war, Brighton racecourse had a racket which deserved the name "protection". Some bookies "welshed" on the bets. Their hired tough accomplices were expected to assault punters trying to collect their winnings while the bookie scarpered with the stake money.

As Roger Mead's crime statistics clearly illustrate, the murder rate in Graham Greene's story which covers two to three weeks is 50% of the entire decade of the nineteen thirties.

CRIME STATISTICS

REPRESENTATIVE OFFENCES REFERRED TO IN GRAHAM GREENE'S NOVEL *BRIGHTON ROCK*.

YEAR	1930	1931	1932	1933	1934	1935	1936	1937	1938	1939
Murder	1	0	0	2	3	0	0	0	1	0
Extortion	0	0	1	0	0	1	0	0	0	1
GBH	1	4	5	1	1	4	6	3	1	3
Prostitution	1	2	3	15	11	11	10	10	2	6
Gambling	52	45	61	30	122	41	75	53	16	6

Source: *Brighton Constabulary Chief Constables Annual Reports 1925-1939*
Used by permission of Roger Mead MA

ROCK & ROLE

"Our interest's on the dangerous edge of things.
the honest thief, the tender murderer,
the superstitious atheist."

ROBERT BROWNING, BISHOP BLOUGHRAM'S APOLOGY

BELOW ROSE, WHO NEVER FORGETS A FACE, SPOTS SPICER'S PHOTOGRAPH UNDER THE BANNER TODAY'S SNAPS CONFIRMING THAT HE IS STILL ALIVE. PINKIE INSISTS THAT THE MAN WHO LEFT THE CARD AT SNOW'S IS DEAD. SOUVENIR PHOTOGRAPHY WAS AN AUTHENTIC ASPECT OF SEASIDE RESORT ENTERTAINMENT.

BRIGHTON ROCK was the novel which attracted to Graham Greene the unwelcome sobriquet 'Catholic writer' although the book published in 1938 had multiple aspects including world politics and murder mystery. Henry Graham Greene had been born in 1904 and baptized into the Church of England.

He was received into the Roman Catholic faith in 1926 while working as a journalist in Nottingham which appears in his fiction as Nottwich. Greene's phenomenal output of novels, film criticism, screenplays, radio & stage plays and correspondence to newspaper editors reveal a preoccupation with religion and its social role which continued until his death in 1991.

LEFT PINKIE RECORDS A WEDDING GIFT FOR ROSE ON THE PALACE PIER SET IN WELWYN STUDIO. HIS POISONOUS MESSAGE INCLUDES THE FILM'S ONLY MENTION OF ROSE'S HOME, NELSON PLACE, A BRIGHTON SLUM STREET DEMOLISHED IN 1937 BEFORE THE PUBLICATION OF THE NOVEL. THE ORIGINAL PHOTO IS A PRODUCTION SNAP USED TO ESTABLISH THE FOCAL DISTANCE FROM THE CAMERA LENS WHICH ACCOUNTS FOR THE GRAINY REPRODUCTION.

Brighton Rock is a great millenarian story with its heart and soul on the slopes of Carlton Hill in a Brighton transformed into a theological battlefield. Graham Greene's work carries a strong sense of his witness to political intrigue and, in this case, to two unconventional churches which may have drawn him into contact with Nelson Place.

From the middle of the 19th century 'Millenarians' anticipated that the promise of the Second Coming of Christ to establish a glorious 1,000 year reign on Earth (referred to as 'the Millennium') might coincide with the distant but approaching end of the year 2,000 Religious tensions arose between churchmen who favoured a Pentecostal direct relationship with the Holy Spirit and moderate factions who supported episcopal authority and the supreme importance of the sacraments.

Within the Church of Scotland's London community, a new extreme sect arose lead by famous preacher Edward Irving who was ultimately accused of heresy. His followers styled themselves the Catholic Apostolic Church and were full of millenarian fervour. A rare Irvingite church was established on the lower slopes of Carlton Hill a suitable Scottish connection as the street was named to commemorate King George IVs 1822 visit to Edinburgh. The long gone church was built in the Early English style in 1865. We can only presume that the congregation was encouraged to "utter" and speak in tongues as did their founding apostle Irving who died aged 42 in 1834.

A short walk uphill past Nelson Place the Mighell Street Hall, on the site now occupied by the American Express European Headquarters, was in use as a Spiritualist Church from 1927. Greene had been

> "From my very first film I was high priest of the mysteries."
> MICHAEL POWELL, FILM MAKER

introduced to spiritualism in 1920 when as a 16 year old schoolboy he went to live for several months at 15 Devonshire Terrace in London with self styled psychoanalyst Kenneth Richmond and his family. Richmond's wife Zoe perceived Greene to be a sensitive 'medium' and felt that writing had deprived the world of his psychic gifts. It is tempting to speculate that Greene was drawn to the churches around Carlton Hill including St. John the Apostle, built for the Church of England but now serving Brighton's Greek Orthodox community.

In noticing and immortalizing Nelson Place Greene misssed a great deal of the reality of life near Carlton Hill. He saw only festering slums where Brighton writer Robert Hayward recalls a warm and welcoming haven, especially for immigrants. Nelson Place was in Brighton's "Latin Quarter" whether or not it housed a high proportion of Roman Catholics and a piece of paradise was just up the hill.

Until 1933 No. 1 Tillbury Place, with its 1.24 acre private garden was the home of Miss Laetitia Tillbury Tarner. Tarnerland Nursery opened the same year and the garden was acquired in 1934. Priory House in Tillbury Place was the newly built Brighton Girl's Club, formerly of Nelson Row which backed on to Nelson Place, in 1936 as Greene began to write his story. Mighell Street still hides a 19th century listed farmhouse behind a rough flint farm wall.

Pinkie and Rose are stripped of their personal histories in the film. Only Prewitt, whom Greene based on the compiler of Old Moore's Almanac, is permitted a past to teach how a privileged boyhood can be blighted by romantic passion. Somewhere between Sussex Street and the hypnotic razzle-dazzle of Palace Pier's 3,000 light bulbs Pinkie lost his baptismal name together with his lost saints, home, parents, godparents and parish. In Greene's imagination did he once walk these streets (then part of the Roman Catholic Diocese of Southwark) with a good Catholic name like Athanasius?

The strong political character of *Brighton Rock* invites contrast with the threatening 1,000 year reich established at Nuremberg in 1933 by Adolf Hitler. Many of Pinkie Brown's memorable traits are shared with the young Hitler: Roman Catholicism, a boyhood vocation to the priesthood, no smoking, no drinking, no sex, vengefulness, a need for scapegoats etc., etc. By 1936 Greene's 1925 debut work *Babbling April* was long forgotten, while it's contemporary *Mein Kamp* was selling 1,000,000 copies a year. The British Board of Film Censors objected to a murderer quoting scripture and required Greene to drop phrases from the Mass, including "He was in the world and the world knew him not." By that time, 1947, the prophetic element of the story no longer

BELOW ENLARGED FRAME STILL. THE VISTA OF CHURCH STREET EXTENDS ACROSS TO CARLTON HILL WHERE THE CATHOLIC APOSTOLIC CHURCH STOOD UNTIL 1964. THIS VIEW TODAY IS FILLED WITH THE DISTINCTIVE AMERICAN EXPRESS HEADQUARTERS.

applied. The co-incidence of Hitler's exceptionally brief marriage and death through suicide pact is somewhat bizzare.

Greene admired Russian writer Feodor Dostoevsky but never could match his experience of prison life. However, he tried to equal the empathy for murderers Dostoevsky expressed in *The Book of the Dead*, "one must tell the truth here these men were exceptional men. Perhaps they were the most gifted, the strongest of our people. But their mighty energies were vainly wasted, wasted abnormally, unjustly, hopelessly. And who was to blame, whose fault was it?" Greene drew Brighton's Pinkie Brown as evil but also as a motherless child, a victim of a moral and spiritual numbness.

American writer Michael Shelden has zeroed in on Greene's interest in crime and proposed him as a suspect for the notorious and still unsolved "Trunk Murder" which drew national attention to Brighton in June 1934. I felt a proper visitor to "Greeneland" when Shelden telephoned to ask if I shared his suspicions. I don't.

ABOVE **RICHARD ATTENBOROUGH, IN COSTUME AS A 13 YEAR OLD SCHOOL BOY, READS *BRIGHTON ROCK* IN THE FIRST UNIFORM EDITION OF GRAHAM GREENE'S NOVELS PUBLISHED IN 1947. ATTENBOROUGH PLAYED THIS ROLE IN THE BOULTING BROTHERS' PRODUCTION *THE GUINEA PIG* WHICH BEGAN FILMING IMMEDIATELY AFTER *BRIGHTON ROCK*. THE PUBLICITY PHOTO WAS NEVER USED.**

Though, oddly, the film draws specific attention to the "Trunk Murder" through its use of time and dates. The movie and novel are generally held to occur circa 1937, a little before the novel was published. But the Brighton Police Report on Fred Hale's death is dated Saturday June 9th so the calendar choices are 1934 or 1945. This completely ignores the novel's references to Whit Monday. Brighton Beach was still a mine field closed to the public in June 1945.

Switching from undetected murder back to religion we find that "*The Rock*", a pageant play written by T. S. Eliot with the purpose of promoting the building of churches in newly developed areas of London, ended its run at Sadler's Well's on Saturday June 9th 1934. Eliot emphasised that, without the spiritual aims set by the Church, modern life is meaningless and empty. So *Brighton Rock*, aside from being a murder weapon in the novel and a simile for human nature in

OPPOSITE **CELEBRITY PORTRAITS WERE IN GREAT DEMAND IN THE 1940s. CAROL MARSH WAS PERMITTED TO LOOK GLAMOUROUS FOR FANS BUT RICHARD ATTENBOROUGH KEPT HIS COSMETIC SCAR, WHICH GAVE THE FILM IT'S US TITLE *YOUNG SCARFACE*.**

the film, may also reflect Brighton's extraordinary Roman Catholic history, especially when it comes to converts. A sly reference to Salome in the novel suggests Aubrey Beardsley who drew poignant pierrots. While writing the screenplay Greene wrote to the Times to protest the defacement of Brighton convert Eric Gill's stone carving of St. Thomas More's monkey in Westminster Cathedral.

Is young Brown "Pinkie Agonistes"? T.S. Eliot famously suggests in his poem *Sweeney Agonistes* that 'any man might do a girl in' and Ida Arnold sounds very Eliotic when she says, "that don't signify" in the pages of the novel.

Young Rose bears the burden of goodness in both the novel and film. Actress Carol Marsh, not long out of Roman Catholic convent school in 1947, feels that she understood and sympathised with the religious symbolism of the film. Rose's tenacious willingness to face eternal damnation with Pinkie wasn't necessarily out of step with its time. In his 1946 novel *Bright Day*, a story of British film actors and their

Hollywood careers, J. B. Priestley admiringly describes a marriageable young woman as one who would follow her husband into hell and back. Greene has Rose offer a touching echo from *The Bible's Book of Ruth*, in her love letter to Pinkie. The Moabite Ruth promised her Jewish husband, "I will go where you go, your people will be my people and your God will be my God."

Graham Greene was adamant that Ida Arnold, the spiritualist, was the unredeemably evil character in *Brighton Rock*. He felt Frank Harvey's stage play might underplay that point. Greene's famous characters offer a contrast between good and evil in Rose and Pinkie. They offer a further contrast between salvation through the grace of the Church of Christ and damnation through direct communication with the souls of the departed. Ida is often labelled an atheist, though spiritualism seeks evidence of survival beyond death, which implies the existence of God. Greene clearly did not welcome the rise of New Age religions.

Pinkie Brown disappears into the sea with no further mention of corpse or funeral rites. The symbolic redemptive power of water had

BELOW CAROL MARSH RELAXES AT WELWYN STUDIO WITH WILLIAM HARTNELL AND WYLIE WATSON WHILE RICHARD ATTENBOROUGH SHAKES HANDS WITH SPICER'S 'STUNT DOUBLE'. THE DAPPER SPIV DALLOW SPORTS A YELLOW CHECK WOOL SUIT, BOW TIE, AND BUTTON SIDED SPATS OVER HIS SHOES. PINKIE'S NATTY SUIT IS BURGUNDY WORN WITH A STRIPPED SHIRT, TARTAN TIE AND SPATS WHICH WENT OUT OF FASHION IN 1939.

often been exploited by Roman Catholic poet Maurice Baring who
died in 1945. His birthday celebrations at the Royal Albion Hotel
ended with a walk into the sea near Palace Pier in full evening dress
fortified with a glass of champagne.

Perhaps St. Peter, the Rock and patron of Brighton and the Church
of Rome mercifully gathers Pinkie's repentant soul from the waters
of Wight into a technicolour purgatory. The ancient wisdom of the
Katha-Upanishad, as Somerset Maugham reminded readers in 1944,
taught that, "The sharp edge of a razor is a difficult thing to pass over;
thus the wise say the path to salvation is hard."

*"the appalling
strangeness of the
mercy of God"*
CHARLES PEGUEY

RIGHT TOUGH GUYS
UNLIMITED EXERCISE
RICHARD ATTENBOROUGH AT
BRIGHTON RACECOURSE.
MICKEY WOODS' STUNT
TEAM WERE ACTIVE AS
COLLEONI'S GANG.

CAST & CREW

Associated British Pictures present The Boulting Brothers' Film *Brighton Rock*.
From the novel by Graham Greene. Made at Welwyn Studios, England. Distributed by Pathe.

CAST

(IN CREDITS ORDER)

Pinkie Brown Richard Attenborough
Ida Arnold Hermione Baddeley
Dallow William Hartnell
Prewitt Harcourt Williams
Spicer Wylie Watson
Cubitt Nigel Stock
Judy Virginia Winter
Frank Reginald Purdell
Phil Corkery George Carney
Fred Hale Alan Wheatley
Colleoni Charles Goldner
Rose Carol Marsh
Molly Lina Barrie
Delia Joan Sterndale-Bennett
Brewer Harry Ross
Police Inspector Campbell Copelin
Waitress Mary Stone
Racecourse Evangelist Norman Watson

Carol Marsh appears by Permission of the
J. Arthur Rank Organization

CREW

Screenplay Graham Greene & Terence Rattigan
Producer Roy Boulting
Director John Boulting
Associate Producer Peter de Sarigny
Composer/Conductor Hans May
Cinematographer Harry Waxman
Costume Design Honoria Plesch
Editor Peter Graham Scott
Sound Editor Audrey Bennett
Production Manager Gerard Bryant
Make Up Artist Bob Clarke
Sound Recordist Frank McNally
Asistant Director Gerry Mitchell
Art Director John Howell
Camera Gilbert Taylor
Song Writer Leslie Julia Jones (More Than Ever)
Arranger Jock Addison (John Addison)

ADDITIONAL CREDITS

CAST

Crooner Constance Smith
Charlie the Barman Carl Ramon
Cosmo Page 1 Ronnie Head
Cosmo Page 2 Billy Batchelor

CREW

Camera Val Stewart
Crowd Marshall George Spence
Hair Polly Richards
Wardrobe Hilda Owen
Visitor Ernest Bevin
Richard Attenborough's
Stunt Double Christopher Law
Stunt Crew Tough Guys Unlimited

Unidentifird speaking roles
Blind Hawker
Trudy Brothers
Barker
Blind Man
Little Girl
Bill the Stallholder
Feathers 'landlord', Jim
Customer
Cosmo Receptionist
Police Detective
Desk Sargent
The Promenaders Pierrot Troupe
Bookies Clerk
Johnnie
Registrar
Policeman
Pier Attendant
Nun

MORALITY TALE

"At the very mention of Brighton most people will immediately think of Brighton Rock, *Graham Greene's gangland novel of the town's more seedy attractions. The book and later the film have become almost as much a part of Brighton's folklore as Prinny and the Pavilion. And for the first time this year the festival boasts a* Brighton Rock *tour taking us round the places real and imaginary and often long gone inhabited by Greene's gallery of villains and victims. I met up with the tour at the station."*

JACK TINKER, MAY 1990. RADIO 2 ARTS PROGRAMME.

"Into this human underworld he had discovered in Brighton, Greene pitched the high Catholic ideas of good and evil, of redemption and grace, to test their spiritual authenticity."

STEPHEN PLAICE, SPLIT ROCK ON THE BRIGHTON ROCK WEB PAGES @ WWW.BRIGHTON.CO. UK/BRIGHTONROCK

JACK TINKER, the late Daily Mail theatre critic described *Brighton Rock* first and foremost as a morality tale. Here are some resources assembled with the help of Father David Wolstenholm to provide hours of meditation for readers inclined to consider the story allegorically.

Morality plays were the poetic liturgical drama of the 15th & 16th centuries derived from Miracle or Mystery plays in which moral themes were presented through male and female allegorical characters such as Everyman and Knowledge. Greene subtitled his film play *The Worst Sin,* a title which still appears on the script issued to cinema projectionists to assist with the reel changes.

Here beginneth a Millennial DIY Treatise how the High Father of Heaven sendeth the Holy Spirit to come and give to every creature wisdom which reveals to the soul that the path to salvation is hard.

Time: Whitsuntide 1937, an intersection with eternity.
Place: Brighton, an imaginary geographical region.

◆ Share out the sins, virtues, gifts and fruits of the Holy Spirit among the characters of *Brighton Rock.*
◆ Expect to find some characteristics distorted like a House of Mirrors.
◆ The Beast no 666 appears courtesy of The Devil, himself.

Seven Deadly Sins: covetousness, pride, lust, envy, gluttony, anger, sloth.

Seven Virtues:(moral virtues) Prudence, Justice, Temperance, Fortitude (theological virtues), Faith, Hope, Charity.

Seven Gifts of the Holy Spirit: Piety, Wisdom, Fear of God, Counsel, Knowledge, Understanding, Fortitude.

Seven Sacraments: Baptism, Penance, Eucharist, Confirmation, Matrimony, Holy Orders, Last Rites.

◆ Read the biblical texts read in Church on Pentecost Sunday:

Morning Deuteronomy XVI to verse 18, second lesson, Acts X verse 34. Evening Isaiah XI, second lesson Acts XIX to verse 21.

Pentecost, which is the seventh Sunday after Easter, celebrates the establishment of the church when the Apostles were filled with the Holy Spirit and given the gift of tongues. Also called Whit or White Sunday, the newly baptized are welcomed into the Church at this time.

The priest wears red (rose red?) vestments on this special feast of the Holy Spirit which opens a week of holy days. Greene used key names repeatedly in his work. Carol Reed's 1949 film *The Fallen Idol* scripted by Greene from his short story *The Basement Room* featured a girl named Rose played by actress Dora Bryan.

BELOW PAGEBOYS RONNIE HEAD AND BILLY BATCHELOR WERE HIRED FROM LEADING LONDON HOTELS TO ADD AUTHENTICITY TO THE COSMOPOLITAN HOTEL SCENES FILMED AT MGM BRITISH STUDIO. PINKIE AND ROSE ARRIVE AS BRIDE AND GROOM WHILE A MESSAGE IS DELIVERED TO THE HAPPY COUPLE ON THE SOFA.

BIBLIOGRAPHY AND FURTHER READING

Backyard Brighton, Queenspark Books No 20.

Baines, Gerald W. *History of the Brighton Police*, 1967.

Carder, Timothy. *The Encyclopedia of Brighton*, ESCC Libraries. 1990.

Burton/O'Sullivan/Wells (eds). *The Family Way*, Flick Books. October 1999.

Falk, Quentin. *Travels in Greeneland*, Quartet Books Ltd. 1984.

Greene, Graham. *Brighton Rock*, Penguin Books. 1973.

Greene, Graham. *A Sort of Life*, Penguin Books. 1972.

Greene, Graham. *Yours, Etc. Letters to the Press 1945-1989*, Penguin Books. 1991.

Greene, Graham. *Ways of Escape*, Penguin Books. 1981.

Hardy, Phil(ed). *The BFI Companion to Crime*, Cassells. 1997.

Hayward, Robert. *Little to Spare & Nothing to Waste*, Brighton Books (Publishing). 1998.

Izod, John. *Hollywood and the Box Office 1895-1986*, MacMillan Press. 1988.

Knowles, David J. *Bitter Sweet Days 1947, A Special Year in Brighton & Sussex*. Knowles Books. September 1999.

MacNab, Geoffrey. *J. Arthur Rank and the British Film Industry*, Routledge. 1993.

Mead, Roger. *A comparative study of the literary Brighton of Graham Greene in his novel* Brighton Rock *with the comtemporary history of the town of Brighton in the 1920's and 1930's*, unpublished Masters Thesis University of Brighton. 1992.

Newsome, David. *The Convert Cardinals Newman and Manning*, John Murray (Publishers) Ltd. 1993.

Noble, Peter(ed). *British Film Yearbook 1947-48*, British Yearbooks Ltd.

Norman, Barry. *Talking Pictures, the story of Hollywood*. Arrow Books Ltd. 1991.

Pertwee, Bill. *Promenades and Pierrots*, Westbridge Books. 1979.

Phillips, Gene D. *Graham Greene: The Films of his Fiction*, Teachers' College Press. 1974.

Priestly, J.B. *Bright Day*, William Heinemann Ltd. 1946.

Shelden, Michael. *The Man Within*, William Heinemann Ltd. 1994.

Sherry, Norman. *The Life of Graham Greene* Volume One, Penguin Books. 1990.

Sherry, Norman. *The Life of Graham Greene* Volume Two, Penguin Books. 1995.

Street, Sarah. *British National Cinema*, Routledge. 1997.

Vincendean, Ginette(ed). *Encyclopedia of European Cinema*, British Film Institute. 1995.

Watts, Cedric. *A Preface to Greene*, Addison Wesley Longman Limited. 1996.

West, W. J. *The Quest for Graham Greene*, Phoenix. 1998.